The Practice of the Presence of God

with
Spiritual Maxims

The Practice of the Presence of God

with
Spiritual Maxims

Brother Lawrence

SPIRE

© 1958, 1967 by Revell

Published by Spire Books
a division of Baker Publishing Group
P.O. Box 6287, Grand Rapids, MI 49516-6287
www.revellbooks.com

ISBN 978-0-8007-8599-4

Printed in the United States of America

12   13   14   15   31   30   29   28   27

CONTENTS

The Practice of the

Presence of God

A PILGRIM'S PRAYER

Lord of all pots and pans and things . . .
Make me a saint by getting meals
And washing up the plates!

Thus Brother Lawrence was able to turn even
the most commonplace and menial task
into a living hymn to the glory of God.

The conversation and letters of this humble
but exalted lay brother have been compiled
to show all of us how, at any moment and
in any circumstance, the soul that seeks the
companionship of God may find Him.

PREFACE

Fame and greatness are relative values and often a delusion and a snare, depending upon circumstances and an attitude of mind. Napoleon was famous to some and infamous to others, and Jesus, crucified in His day, is greater with the passing years. Perhaps the greatest of men are those who never seek greatness at all, but who personify the virtues which posterity calls great. Such an one was Brother Lawrence, known largely to posterity by way of the beauty of this little book, beloved to succeeding generations not as king or conqueror or Croesus but because, with a mind so like the mind which was in Christ, he lived so abundantly in the presence of God.

The value of this book lies in its Christian humility and simplicity. No conceited scholar was Brother Lawrence; theological and doctrinal debates bored him, if he noticed them at all. His one desire was for communion with God. We find him worshiping more in his kitchen than in his cathedral; he could pray, with another

Lord of all pots and pans and things . . .
Make me a saint by getting meals
And washing up the plates!

11

and he could say, "The time of business does not with me differ from the time of prayer, and in the noise and clatter of my kitchen, while several persons are at the same time calling for different things, I possess God in as great tranquillity as if I were upon my knees at the blessed sacrament."

Except for the kitchen, we know little of his career: only that he was born Nicholas Herman in French Lorraine, that he was lowly and unlearned in the teaching of the schools, that he served briefly as footman and soldier, and under the whips of God and conscience was driven to become a lay brother among the barefooted Carmelites at Paris in the year 1666 and was known forever after that as "Brother Lawrence." His conversion, at eighteen, was the result of the mere sight on a midwinter day of a dry and leafless tree standing gaunt against the snow; it stirred deep thoughts within him of the change the coming spring would bring. From that moment on he grew and waxed strong in the knowledge and love and favor of God, endeavoring constantly, as he put it, "to walk as in His presence." No wilderness wanderings, no bitter winter seasons of soul or spirit, seem to have intervened between the Red Sea and the Jordan of his experience. A wholly consecrated man, he lived his life as though he were a singing pilgrim on the march, as happy in serving his fellow monks and

brothers from the monastery kitchen as in serving
God in the vigil of prayer and penance. He died at
eighty years of age, full of love and years and
honored by all who knew him, leaving a name
which has been "as precious ointment poured
forth."

This little record of his mind and heart is made up
of notes of several conversations with him and
letters written by him, set in order by M. Beaufort,
grand vicar to M. de Chalons, formerly Cardinal de
Noailles, by whose recommendation the "Letters"
were first published. The whole world has received
it gladly; no man lives who knows how many
editions there have been, how many millions have
read these words. That was to be expected, for here
is a wisdom which only lips that have been touched
by the Lord can express, and truth and faith and
love and hope for which the hearts of ages of men
have longed.

We publish it as a unique record of one who
walked with Christ because he chose to walk among
the lowly, of one who saw God's glory shining in
the commonplace. Wherever he was, the Light was
there; wherever he walked was hallowed ground.
He showed us how, at any moment and in any
circumstance, the soul that seeks God may find
Him, and practice the presence of God.

Such a story, such an accomplishment, should

never die, so long as there are those who spend lifetimes in quest of the assurance and the wisdom of the lowly lay brother of Paris.

THE PUBLISHERS

CONVERSATIONS

The first time I saw brother Lawrence was upon the third of August, 1666. He told me that God had done him a singular favor in his conversion at the age of eighteen.

That in the winter, seeing a tree stripped of its leaves, and considering that within a little time the leaves would be renewed, and after that the flowers and fruit appear, he received a high view of the providence and power of God, which has never since been effaced from his soul. That this view had perfectly set him loose from the world, and kindled in him such a love for God that he could not tell whether it had increased during the more than forty years he had lived since.

That he had been footman to M. Fieubert, the treasurer, and that he was a great awkward fellow who broke everything.

That he had desired to be received into a monastery, thinking that he would there be made to smart for his awkwardness and the faults he should commit, and so he should sacrifice to God his life, with its pleasures; but that God had disappointed him, he having met with nothing but satisfaction in that state.

That we should establish ourselves in a sense of God's presence by continually conversing with Him. That it was a shameful thing to quit His conversation to think of trifles and fooleries.

That we should feed and nourish our souls with high notions of God, which would yield us great joy in being devoted to Him.

That we ought to quicken—i.e., to enliven—our faith. That it was lamentable we had so little; and that instead of taking *faith* for the rule of their conduct, men amused themselves with trivial devotions, which changed daily. That the way of faith was the spirit of the church, and that it was sufficient to bring us to a high degree of perfection.

That we ought to give ourselves up to God, with regard both to things temporal and spiritual, and seek our satisfaction only in the fulfilling of His will, whether He lead us by suffering or by consolation, for all would be equal to a soul truly resigned. That there needed fidelity in those drynesses or insensibilities and irksomenesses in prayer by which God tries our love to Him; that *then* was the time for us to make good and effectual acts of resignation, whereof one alone would oftentimes very much promote our spiritual advancement.

That as for the miseries and sins he heard of daily in the world, he was so far from wondering at them that, on the contrary, he was surprised that there were not more, considering the malice sinners were capable of; that, for his part, he prayed for them; but knowing that God could remedy the mischiefs they did when He pleased, he gave himself no further trouble.

That to arrive at such resignation as God requires, we should watch attentively over all the passions which mingle as well in spiritual things as in those of a grosser nature; that God would give light concerning those passions to those who truly desire to serve Him. That if this was my design, sincerely to serve God, I might come to him (Brother Lawrence) as often as I pleased, without any fear of being troublesome; but if not, that I ought no more to visit him.

SECOND CONVERSATION

That he had always been governed by love, without selfish views; and that having resolved to make the love of God the *end* of all his actions, he had found reasons to be well satisfied with his method. That he was pleased when he could take up a straw from the ground for the love of God, seeking Him only, and nothing else, not even His gifts.

That he had been long troubled in mind from a certain belief that he should be damned; that all the men in the world could not have persuaded him to the contrary; but that he had thus reasoned with himself about it: *I engaged in a religious life only for the love of God, and I have endeavored to act only for Him; whatever becomes of me, whether I be lost or saved, I will always continue to act purely for the love of God. I shall have this good at least, that till death I shall have done all that is in me to love Him.* That this trouble of mind had lasted four years, during which time he had suffered much; but that at last he had seen that this trouble arose from want of faith, and that since he had passed his life in perfect liberty and continual joy. That he had placed his sins betwixt him and God, as it were, to tell Him that he did not deserve His favors, but that God still continued to bestow them in abundance.

That in order to form a habit of conversing with God continually, and referring all we do to Him, we must first apply to Him with some diligence; but that after a little care we should find His love inwardly excite us to it without any difficulty.

That he expected, after the pleasant days God had given him, he should have his turn of pain and suffering; but that he was not uneasy about it, knowing very well that as he could do nothing of himself, God would not fail to give Him the strength to bear it.

That when an occasion of practicing some virtue offered, he addressed himself to God, saying, *Lord, I cannot do this unless Thou enablest me;* and that then he received strength more than sufficient.

That when he had failed in his duty, he only confessed his fault, saying to God, *I shall never do otherwise if You leave me to myself; it is You who must hinder my falling and mend what is amiss.* That after this he gave himself no further uneasiness about it.

That we ought to act with God in the greatest simplicity, speaking to Him frankly and plainly, and imploring His assistance in our affairs, just as they happen. That God never failed to grant it, as he had often experienced.

That he had been lately sent into Burgundy, to buy the provision of wine for the society, which was a very unwelcome task for him, because he had no turn for business, and because he was lame and could not go about the boat but by rolling himself over the casks. That, however, he gave himself no uneasiness about it, nor about the purchase of the wine. That he said to God it was His business he was about, and that he afterward found it very well performed. That he had been sent into Auvergne, the year before, upon the same account; that he could not tell how the matter passed, but that it proved very well.

So, likewise, in his business in the kitchen (to which he had naturally a great aversion), having accustomed himself to do everything there for the love of God, and with prayer, upon all occasions, for His grace to do his work well, he had found everything easy, during fifteen years that he had been employed there.

That he was very well pleased with the post he was now in; but that he was as ready to quit that as the former, since he was always pleasing to himself in every condition by doing little things for the love of God.

That with him the set times of prayer were not different from other times; that he retired to pray, according to the directions of his superior, but that he did not want such retirement, nor ask for it, because his greatest business did not divert him from God.

That as he knew his obligation to love God in all things, and as he endeavored so to do, he had no need of a director to advise him, but that he needed much a confessor to absolve him. That he was very sensible of his faults, but not discouraged by them; that he confessed them to God, but did not plead against Him to excuse them. When he had so done, he peaceably resumed his usual practice of love and adoration.

That in his trouble of mind he had consulted

nobody, but knowing only by the light of faith that God was present, he contented himself with directing all his actions to Him, i.e., doing them with a desire to please Him, let what would come of it.

That useless thoughts spoil all; that the mischief began there; but that we ought to reject them as soon as we perceived their impertinence to the matter in hand, or our salvation, and return to our communion with God.

That at the beginning he had often passed his time appointed for prayer in rejecting wandering thoughts and falling back into them. That he could never regulate his devotion by certain methods as some do. That, nevertheless, at first he had *meditated* for some time, but afterward that went off, in a manner he could give no account of.

That all bodily mortifications and other exercises are useless, except as they serve to arrive at the union with God by love; that he had well considered this, and found it the shortest way to go straight to Him by a continual exercise of love and doing all things for His sake.

That we ought to make a great difference between the acts of the understanding and those of the will; that the first were comparatively of little value, and the others, all. That our only business was to love and delight ourselves in God.

That all possible kinds of mortification, if they

were void of the love of God, could not efface a single sin. That we ought, without anxiety, to expect the pardon of our sins from the blood of Jesus Christ, only endeavoring to love Him with all our hearts. That God seemed to have granted the greatest favors to the greatest sinners, as more signal monuments of His mercy.

That the greatest pains or pleasures of this world were not to be compared with what he had experienced of both kinds in a spiritual state; so that he was careful for nothing and feared nothing, desiring only one thing of God, viz., that he might not offend Him.

That he had no scruples; for, said he, when I fail in my duty, I readily acknowledge it, saying, *I am used to do so; I shall never do otherwise if I am left to myself.* If I fail not, then I give God thanks, acknowledging that the strength comes from Him.

THIRD CONVERSATION

He told me that the foundation of the spiritual life in him had been a high notion and esteem of God in faith; which when he had once well conceived, he had no other care at first but faithfully to reject every other thought, *that he might perform all his actions for the love of God.* That when sometimes he had not thought of God for a good while, he did not disquiet himself for it; but, after having acknowledged his wretchedness to God, he returned to Him with so much the greater trust in Him as he had found himself wretched through forgetting Him.

That the trust we put in God honors Him much and draws down great graces.

That it was impossible not only that God should deceive, but also that He should long let a soul suffer which is perfectly resigned to Him, and resolved to endure everything for His sake.

That he had so often experienced the ready succors of divine grace upon all occasions, that from the same experience, when he had business to do, he did not think of it beforehand; but when it was time to do it, he found in God, as in a clear mirror, all that was fit for him to do. That of late he had acted thus, without anticipating care; but before the experience above mentioned, he had used it in his affairs.

When outward business diverted him a little from the thought of God, a fresh remembrance coming from God invested his soul, and so inflamed and transported him that it was difficult for him to contain himself.

That he was more united to God in his outward employments than when he left them for devotion and retirement.

That he expected hereafter some great pain of body or mind; that the worst that could happen to him was to lose that sense of God which he had enjoyed so long; but that the goodness of God assured him He would not forsake him utterly, and that He would give him strength to bear whatever evil He permitted to happen to him; and therefore that he feared nothing, and had no occasion to consult with anybody about his state. That when he had attempted to do it, he had always come away more perplexed; and that as he was conscious of his readiness to lay down his life for the love of God, he had no apprehension of danger. That perfect resignation to God was a sure way to heaven, a way in which he had always sufficient light for our conduct.

That in the beginning of the spiritual life we ought to be faithful in doing our duty and denying ourselves; but after that, unspeakable pleasures followed. That in difficulties we need only have recourse to Jesus Christ, and beg His grace; with that everything became easy.

That many do not advance in the Christian progress because they stick in penances and particular exercises, while they neglect the love of God, which is the *end*. That this appeared plainly by their works, and was the reason why we see so little solid virtue.

That there needed neither art nor science for

going to God, but only a heart resolutely determined
to apply itself to nothing but Him, or for His sake,
and to love Him only.

FOURTH CONVERSATION

He discoursed with me frequently, and with great
openness of heart, concerning his manner of *going*
to God, whereof some part is related already.

He told me that all consists in one hearty renun-
ciation of everything which we are sensible does not
lead to God. That we might accustom ourselves to a
continual conversation with Him, with freedom and
in simplicity. That we need only to recognize God
intimately present with us, to address ourselves to
Him every moment, that we may beg His assistance
for knowing His will in things doubtful, and for
rightly performing those which we plainly see He
requires of us, offering them to Him before we do
them, and giving Him thanks when we have done.

That in this conversation with God we are also
employed in praising, adoring, and loving Him incessantly, for His infinite goodness and perfection.

That, without being discouraged on account of our
sins, we should pray for His grace with a perfect
confidence, as relying upon the infinite merits of our
Lord Jesus Christ. That God never failed offering us
His grace at each action; that he distinctly perceived

it, and never failed of it, unless when his thoughts had wandered from a sense of God's presence, or he had forgotten to ask His assistance.

That God always gave us light in our doubts when we had no other design but to please Him.

That our sanctification did not depend upon *changing* our works, but in doing that for God's sake which we commonly do for our own. That it was lamentable to see how many people mistook the means for the end, addicting themselves to certain works, which they performed very imperfectly, by reason of their human or selfish regards.

That the most excellent method he had found of going to God was that of doing our common business without any view of pleasing men,* and (as far we are capable) purely for the love of God.

That it was a great delusion to think that the times of prayer ought to differ from other times; that we are as strictly obliged to adhere to God by action in the time of action as by prayer in the season of prayer.

That his prayer was nothing else but a sense of the presence of God, his soul being at that time insensible to everything but divine love; and that when the appointed times of prayer were past, he found no difference, because he still continued with God, praising and blessing Him with all his might, so that he passed his life in continual joy; yet hoped

* Gal. 1:10; Eph. 6:5, 6.

that God would give him somewhat to suffer when he should grow stronger.

That we ought, once for all, heartily to put our whole trust in God, and make a total surrender of ourselves to Him, secure that He would not deceive us.

That we ought not to be weary of doing little things for the love of God, who regards not the greatness of the work, but the love with which it is performed. That we should not wonder if, in the beginning, we often failed in our endeavors, but that at last we should gain a habit, which will naturally produce its acts in us, without our care, and to our exceeding great delight.

That the whole substance of religion was faith, hope, and charity, by the practice of which we become united to the will of God; that all besides is indifferent, and to be used as a means that we may arrive at our end, and be swallowed up therein, by faith and charity.

That all things are possible to him who *believes;* that they are less difficult to him who *hopes;* that they are more easy to him who *loves* and still more easy to him who perseveres in the practice of these three virtues.

That the end we ought to propose to ourselves is to become, in this life, the most perfect worshipers of God we can possibly be, as we hope to be through all eternity.

That when we enter upon the spiritual life, we should consider and examine to the bottom what we are. And then we should find ourselves worthy of all contempt, and not deserving indeed the name of Christians; subject to all kinds of misery and numberless accidents, which trouble us and cause perpetual vicissitudes in our health, in our humors, in our internal and external dispositions; in fine, persons whom God would humble by many pains and labors, as well within as without. After this we should not wonder that troubles, temptations, oppositions, and contradictions happen to us from men. We ought, on the contrary, to submit ourselves to them, and bear them as long as God pleases, as things highly advantageous to us.

That the greater perfection a soul aspires after, the more dependent it is upon divine grace.

*Being questioned by one of his own society (to whom he was obliged to open himself) by what means he had attained such an habitual sense of God, he told him that, since his first coming to the monastery, he had considered God as the end of all his thoughts and desires, as the mark to which they should tend, and in which they should terminate.

That in the beginning of his novitiate he spent the hours appointed for private prayer in thinking of

* The particulars which follow are collected from other accounts of Brother Lawrence.

God, so as to convince his mind of, and to impress deeply upon his heart, the divine existence, rather by devout sentiments, and submission to the lights of faith, than by studied reasonings and elaborate meditations. That by this short and sure method he exercised himself in the knowledge and love of God, resolving to use his utmost endeavor to live in a continual sense of His presence, and, if possible never to forget Him more.

That when he had thus in prayer filled his mind with great sentiments of that infinite Being, he went to his work appointed in the kitchen (for he was cook to the society). There having first considered severally the things his office required, and when and how each thing was to be done, he spent all the intervals of his time, as well before as after his work, in prayer.

That when he began his business, he said to God, with a filial trust in Him: *O my God, since Thou art with me, and I must now, in obedience to Thy commands, apply my mind to these outward things, I beseech Thee to grant me the grace to continue in Thy presence; and to this end do Thou prosper me with Thy assistance, receive all my works, and possess all my affections.*

As he proceeded in his work he continued his familiar conversation with his Maker, imploring His grace, and offering to Him all his actions.

When he had finished he examined himself how he had discharged his duty; if he found *well,* he returned thanks to God; if otherwise, he asked pardon, and, without being discouraged, he set his mind right again, and continued his exercise of the *presence* of God as if he had never deviated from it. "Thus," said he, "by rising after my falls, and by frequently renewed acts of faith and love, I am come to a state wherein it would be as difficult for me not to think of God as it was at first to accustom myself to it."

As Brother Lawrence had found such an advantage in walking in the presence of God, it was natural for him to recommend it earnestly to others; but his example was a stronger inducement than any arguments he could propose. His very countenance was edifying, such a sweet and calm devotion appearing in it as could not but affect the beholders. And it was observed that in the greatest hurry of business in the kitchen he still preserved his recollection and heavenly-mindedness. He was never hasty nor loitering, but did each thing in its season, with an even, uninterrupted composure and tranquillity of spirit. "The time of business," said he, "does not with me differ from the time of prayer; and in the noise and clatter of my kitchen, while several persons are at the same time calling for different things, I possess God in as great tranquillity as if I were upon my knees at the blessed sacrament."

LETTERS

Since you desire so earnestly that I should communicate to you the method by which I arrived at that *habitual sense of God's presence,* which our Lord, of His mercy, has been pleased to vouchsafe to me, I must tell you that it is with great difficulty that I am prevailed on by your importunities; and now I do it only upon the terms that you show my letter to nobody. If I knew that you would let it be seen, all the desire that I have for your advancement would not be able to determine me to it. The account I can give you is:

Having found in many books different methods of going to God, and divers practices of the spiritual life, I thought this would serve rather to puzzle me than facilitate what I sought after, which was nothing but how to become wholly God's. This made me resolve to give the all for the all; so after having given myself wholly to God, that He might take away my sin, I renounced, for the love of Him, everything that was not He, and I began to live as if there was none but He and I in the world. Sometimes I considered myself before Him as a poor criminal at the feet of his judge; at other times I beheld Him in my heart as my Father, as my God. I worshiped Him the oftenest that I could, keeping my mind in His holy presence, and recalling it as often as I found it wandered from Him. I found no small pain in this exercise, and yet I continued it, notwithstanding all the difficulties that occurred, without troubling or disquieting myself when my mind had wandered involuntarily. I made this my business as much all the day long as at the appointed times of prayer; for at all times, every hour, every minute, even in the height of my business, I drove away from my mind everything that was capable of interrupting my thought of God.

Such has been my common practice ever since I entered in religion; and though I have done it very imperfectly, yet I have found great advantages by it. These, I well know, are to be imputed to the mere mercy and goodness of God, because we can do nothing without Him, and I still less than any. But when we are faithful to keep ourselves in His holy presence, and set Him always before us, this not only hinders our offending Him and doing anything that may displease Him, at least wilfully, but it also begets in us a holy freedom, and, if I may so speak, a familiarity with God, wherewith we ask, and that successfully, the graces we stand in need of. In fine, by often repeating these acts, they become habitual, and the presence of God rendered as it were natural to us. Give Him thanks, if you please, with me, for His great goodness toward me, which I can never sufficiently admire, for the many favors He has done to so miserable a sinner as I am. May all things praise Him. Amen.

I am, in our Lord,

Yours . . .

SECOND LETTER

To the Reverend—

Not finding my manner of life in books, although I have no difficulty about it, yet, for greater security, I shall be glad to know your thoughts concerning it.

In a conversation some days since with a person of piety, he told me the spiritual life was a life of grace, which begins with servile fear, which is increased by hope of eternal life, and which is consummated by pure love; that each of these states had its different stages, by which one arrives at last at that blessed consummation.

I have not followed all these methods. On the contrary, from I know not what instincts, I found they discouraged me. This was the reason why, at my entrance into religion, I took a resolution to give myself up to God, as the best return I could make for His love, and, for the love of Him, to renounce all besides.

For the first year I commonly employed myself during the time set apart for devotion with the thought of death, judgment, heaven, hell, and my sins. Thus I continued some years, applying my mind carefully the rest of the day, and even in the midst of my business, *to the presence of God,* whom I considered always as *with* me, often as *in* me.

At length I came insensibly to do the same thing during my set time of prayer, which caused in me great delight and consolation. This practice produced in me so high an esteem for God that faith alone was capable to satisfy me in that point.*

Such was my beginning, and yet I must tell you that for the first ten years I suffered much. The apprehension that I was not devoted to God as I wished to be, my past sins always present to my mind, and the great unmerited favors which God did me, were the matter and source of my sufferings. During this time I fell often, and rose again presently. It seemed to me that all creatures, reason, and God Himself were against me, and faith alone

---

* I suppose he means that all distinct notions he could form of God were unsatisfactory, because he perceived them to be unworthy of God; and therefore his mind was not to be satisfied but by the views of faith, which apprehend God as infinite and incomprehensible, as He is in Himself, and not as He can be conceived by human ideas.

for me. I was troubled sometimes with thoughts that to believe I had received such favors was an effect of my presumption, which pretended to be at once where others arrive with difficulty; at other times, that it was a wilful delusion, and that there was no salvation for me.

When I thought of nothing but to end my days in these troubles (which did not at all diminish the trust I had in God, and which served only to increase my faith), I found myself changed all at once; and my soul, which till that time was in trouble, felt a profound inward peace, as if she were in her center and place of rest.

Ever since that time I walked before God, simply, in faith, with humility and with love, and I apply myself diligently to do nothing and think nothing which may displease Him. I hope that when I have done what I can, He will do with me what He pleases.

As for what passes in me at present, I cannot express it. I have no pain or difficulty about my state, because I have no will but that of God, which I endeavor to accomplish in all things, and to which I am so resigned that I would not take up a straw from the ground against His order, or from any other motive than purely that of love to Him.

I have quitted all forms of devotion and set prayers but those to which my state obliges me.

And I make it my business only to persevere in His holy presence, wherein I keep myself by a simple attention, and a general fond regard to God, which I may call an *actual presence* of God; or, to speak better, an habitual, silent, and secret conversation of the soul with God, which often causes me joys and raptures inwardly, and sometimes also outwardly, so great that I am forced to use means to moderate them and prevent their appearance to others.

In short, I am assured beyond all doubt that my soul has been with God above these thirty years. I pass over many things that I may not be tedious to you, yet I think it proper to inform you after what manner I consider myself before God, whom I behold as my King.

I consider myself as the most wretched of men, full of sores and corruption, and who has committed all sorts of crimes against his King. Touched with a sensible regret, I confess to Him all my wickedness, I ask His forgiveness, I abandon myself in His hands that He may do what He pleases with me. The King, full of mercy and goodness, very far from chastising me, embraces me with love, makes me eat at His table, serves me with His own hands, gives me the key of His treasures; He converses and delights Himself with me incessantly, in a thousand and a thousand ways, and treats me in all respects as His favorite. It is thus I consider myself from time to time in His holy presence.

My most useful method is this simple attention, and such a general passionate regard to God, to whom I find myself often attached with greater sweetness and delight than that of an infant at the mother's breast; so that, if I dare use the expression, I should choose to call this state the bosom of God, for the inexpressible sweetness which I taste and experience there.

If sometimes my thoughts wander from it by necessity or infirmity, I am presently recalled by inward motions so charming and delicious that I am ashamed to mention them. I desire your reverence to reflect rather upon my great wretchedness, of which you are fully informed, than upon the great favors which God does me, all unworthy and ungrateful as I am.

As for my set hours of prayer, they are only a continuation of the same exercise. Sometimes I consider myself there as a stone before a carver, whereof he is to make a statue; presenting myself thus before God, I desire Him to form His perfect image in my soul, and make me entirely like Himself.

At other times, when I apply myself to prayer, I feel all my spirit and all my soul lift itself up without any care or effort of mine, and it continues as it were suspended and firmly fixed in God, as in its center and place of rest.

I know that some charge this state with inactivity, delusion, and self-love. I confess that it is a holy inactivity, and would be a happy self-love if the soul in that state were capable of it, because, in effect, while she is in this repose, she cannot be disturbed by such acts as she was formerly accustomed to, and which were then her support, but which would now rather hinder than assist her.

Yet I cannot bear that this should be called delusion, because the soul which thus enjoys God desires herein nothing but Him. If this be delusion in me, it belongs to God to remedy it. Let Him do what He pleases with me; I desire only Him, and to be wholly devoted to Him. You will, however, oblige me in sending me your opinion, to which I always pay a great deference, for I have a singular esteem for your reverence, and am, in our Lord,

Yours . . .

THIRD LETTER

We have a God who is infinitely gracious and knows all about our wants. I always thought that He would reduce you to extremity. He will come in His own time, and when you least expect it. Hope in

Him more than ever; thank Him with me for the favors He does you, particularly for the fortitude and patience which He gives you in your afflictions. It is a plain mark of the care He takes of you. Comfort yourself, then, with Him, and give thanks for all.

I admire also the fortitude and bravery of Mr.—. God has given him a good disposition and a good will; but there is in him still a little of the world and a great deal of youth. I hope the affliction which God has sent him will prove a wholesome remedy to him, and make him enter into himself. It is an accident which should engage him to put all his trust in *Him* who accompanies him everywhere. Let him think of Him as often as he can, especially in the greatest dangers. A little lifting up of the heart suffices. A little remembrance of God, one act of inward worship, though upon a march, and a sword in hand, are prayers, which however short, are nevertheless very acceptable to God; and far from lessening a soldier's courage in occasions of danger, they best serve to fortify it.

Let him then think of God the most he can. Let him accustom himself, by degrees, to this small but holy exercise. No one will notice it, and nothing is easier than to repeat often in the day these little internal adorations. Recommend to him, if you please, that he think of God the most he can, in the manner here directed. It is very fit and most necessary for a soldier who is daily exposed to the dangers of life. I hope that God will assist him and all the family, to whom I present my service, being theirs and

                                    Yours . . .

FOURTH LETTER

I have taken this opportunity to communicate to you the sentiments of one of our society, concerning the admirable effects and continual assistances which he receives from *the presence of God*. Let you and me both profit by them.

You must know his continual care has been, for about forty years past that he has spent in religion, to be always with God, and to do nothing, say nothing, and think nothing which may displease Him, and this without any other view than purely for the love of Him, and because He deserves infinitely more.

He is now so accustomed to that divine presence that he receives from it continual succors upon all occasions. For about thirty years his soul has been filled with joys so continual, and sometimes so great, that he is forced to use means to moderate them, and to hinder their appearing outwardly.

If sometimes he is a little too much absent from that divine presence, God presently makes Himself to be felt in his soul to recall him, which often happens when he is most engaged in his outward business. He answers with exact fidelity to these inward drawings, either by an elevation of his heart toward God, or by a meek and fond regard to Him; or by such words as love forms upon these occasions, as, for instance, *My God, here I am all devoted to thee. Lord, make me according to Thy heart.* And then it seems to him (as in effect he feels it) that this God of love, satisfied with such few words, reposes again, and rests in the fund and center of his soul. The experience of these things gives him such an assurance that God is always in the fund or bottom of his soul that it renders him incapable of doubting it upon any account whatever.

Judge by this what content and satisfaction he enjoys while he continually finds in himself so great a treasure. He is no longer in an anxious search after it, but has it open before him, and may take what he pleases of it.

He complains much of our blindness, and cries often that we are to be pitied who content ourselves with so little. *God,* saith he, *has infinite treasure to bestow, and we take up with a little sensible devotion, which passes in a moment. Blind as we are, we hinder God and stop the current of His graces. But when He finds a soul penetrated with a lively faith, He pours into it His graces and favors plentifully; there they flow like a torrent which, after being forcibly stopped against its ordinary course, when it has found a passage, spreads itself with impetuosity and abundance.*

Yes, we often stop this torrent by the little value we set upon it. But let us stop it no more; let us enter into ourselves and break down the bank which hinders it. Let us make way for grace; let us redeem the lost time, for perhaps we have but little left. Death follows us close; let us be well prepared for it; for we die but once, and a miscarriage there is irretrievable.

I say again, let us enter into ourselves. The time presses, there is no room for delay; our souls are at stake. I believe you have taken such effectual measures that you will not be surprised. I commend you for it; it is the one thing necessary. We must, nevertheless, always work at it, because not to advance in the spiritual life is to go back. But those who have the gale of the Holy Spirit go forward even in sleep. If the vessel of our soul is still tossed with winds and storms, let us awake the Lord, who reposes in it, and He will quickly calm the sea.

I have taken the liberty to impart to you these good sentiments, that you may compare them with your own. It will serve again to kindle and inflame them, if by misfortune (which God forbid, for it would be indeed a great misfortune) they should be, though never so little, cooled. Let us then both recall our first fervors. Let us profit by the example and the sentiments of this brother, who is little known of the world, but known of God, and extremely caressed by Him. I will pray for you; do you pray instantly for me, who am, in our Lord,

Yours . . .

FIFTH LETTER

I received this day two books and a letter from Sister—, who is preparing to make her profession, and upon that account desires the prayers of your holy society, and yours in particular. I perceive that she reckons much upon them; pray do not disappoint her. Beg of God that she may make her sacrifice in the view of His love alone, and with a firm resolution to be wholly devoted to Him. I will send you one of these books, which treat of the presence of God, a subject which, in my opinion, contains the whole spiritual life; and it seems to me that whoever duly practices it will soon become spiritual.

I know that for the right practice of it the heart

must be empty of all other things, because God will possess the heart *alone;* and as He cannot possess it alone without emptying it of all besides, so neither can He act there, and do in it what He pleases, unless it be left vacant to Him.

There is not in the world a kind of life more sweet and delightful than that of a continual conversation with God. Those only can comprehend it who practice and experience it; yet I do not advise you to do it from that motive. It is not pleasure which we ought to seek in this exercise; but let us do it from a principle of love, and because God would have us.

Were I a preacher, I should, above all other things, preach the practice of the presence of God; and were I a director, I should advise all the world to do it, so necessary do I think it, and so easy, too.

Ah! knew we but the want we have of the grace and assistance of God, we should never lose sight of Him—no, not for a moment. Believe me; make immediately a holy and firm resolution nevermore wilfully to forget Him, and to spend the rest of your days in His sacred presence, deprived, for the love of Him, if He thinks fit, of all consolations.

Set heartily about this work, and if you do it as you ought, be assured that you will find the effects of it. I will assist you with my prayers, poor as they are. I recommend myself earnestly to yours and those of your holy society, being theirs, and more particularly

Yours . . .

SIXTH LETTER

(To the Same)

I have received from Mrs.— the things which you gave her for me. I wonder that you have not given me your thoughts of the little book I sent to you, and which you must have received. Pray set heartily about the practice of it in your old age; it is better late than never.

I cannot imagine how religious persons can live satisfied without the practice of the presence of God. For my part, I keep myself retired with Him in the fund or center of my soul as much as I can; and while I am so with Him I fear nothing, but the least turning from Him is insupportable.

This exercise does not much fatigue the body; it is, however, proper to deprive it sometimes, nay, often, of many little pleasures which are innocent and lawful, for God will not permit that a soul which desires to be devoted entirely to Him should take other pleasures than with Him: that is more than reasonable.

I do not say that therefore we must put any violent

constraint upon ourselves. No, we must serve God in a holy freedom; we must do our business faithfully, without trouble or disquiet, recalling our mind to God mildly, and with tranquillity, as often as we find it wandering from Him.

It is, however, necessary to put our whole trust in God, laying aside all other cares, and even some particular forms of devotion, though very good in themselves, yet such as one often engages in unreasonably, because these devotions are only means to attain to the end. So when by this exercise of the presence of God we are *with Him* who is our end, it is then useless to return to the means; but we may continue with Him our commerce of love, persevering in His holy presence, one while by an act of praise, of adoration, or of desire; one while by an act of resignation or thanksgiving; and in all the ways which our spirit can invent.

Be not discouraged by the repugnance which you may find in it from nature; you must do yourself violence. At the first one often thinks it lost time, but you must go on, and resolve to persevere in it to death, notwithstanding all the difficulties that may occur. I recommend myself to the prayers of your holy society, and yours in particular. I am, in our Lord,

Yours . . .

SEVENTH LETTER

I pity you much. It will be of great importance if you can leave the care of your affairs to—, and spend the remainder of your life only in worshiping God. He requires no great matters of us: a little remembrance of Him from time to time; a little adoration; sometimes to pray for His grace, sometimes to offer Him your sufferings, and sometimes to return Him thanks for the favors He has given you, and still gives you, in the midst of your troubles, and to console yourself with Him the oftenest you can. Lift up your heart to Him, sometimes even at your meals, and when you are in company; the least little remembrance will always be acceptable to Him. You need not cry very loud; He is nearer to us than we are aware of.

It is not necessary for being with God to be always at church. We may make an oratory of our heart wherein to retire from time to time to converse with Him in meekness, humility, and love. Every one is capable of such familiar conversation with God, some more, some less. He knows what we can do. Let us begin, then. Perhaps He expects but one generous resolution on our part. Have courage. We have but little time to live; you are near sixty-four, and I am almost eighty. Let us live and die with God.

Sufferings will be sweet and pleasant to us while we are with Him; and the greatest pleasures will be, without Him, a cruel punishment to us. May He be blessed for all. Amen.

Accustom yourself, then, by degrees thus to worship Him, to beg His grace, to offer Him your heart from time to time in the midst of your business, even every moment, if you can. Do not always scrupulously confine yourself to certain rules, or particular forms of devotion, but act with a general confidence in God, with love and humility. You may assure—of my poor prayers, and that I am their servant, and particularly

Yours in our Lord . . .

EIGHTH LETTER

(*Concerning Wandering Thoughts in Prayer*)

You tell me nothing new; you are not the only one that is troubled with wandering thoughts. Our mind is extremely roving; but, as the will is mistress of all our faculties, she must recall them, and carry them to God as their last end.

When the mind, for want of being sufficiently reduced by recollection at our first engaging in devotion, has contracted certain bad habits of wandering and dissipation, they are difficult to overcome, and commonly draw us, even against our wills, to the things of the earth.

I believe one remedy for this is to confess our faults and to humble ourselves before God. I do not advise you to use multiplicity of words in prayer, many words and long discourses being often the occasions of wandering. Hold yourself in prayer before God like a dumb or paralytic beggar at a rich man's gate. Let it be your business to keep your mind in the presence of the Lord. If it sometimes wander and withdraw itself from Him, do not much disquiet yourself for that: trouble and disquiet serve rather to distract the mind than to recollect it; the will must bring it back in tranquillity. If you persevere in this manner, God will have pity on you.

One way to recollect the mind easily in the time of prayer, and preserve it more in tranquillity, is *not to let it wander too far at other times*. You should keep it strictly in the presence of God; and being accustomed to think of Him often, you will find it easy to keep your mind calm in the time of prayer, or at least to recall it from its wanderings.

I have told you already at large, in my former letters, of the advantages we may draw from this practice of the presence of God. Let us set about seriously, and pray for one another.

Yours . . .

NINTH LETTER

The enclosed is an answer to that which I received from—; pray deliver it to her. She seems to me full of good will, but she would go faster than grace. One does not become holy all at once. I recommend her to you; we ought to help one another by our advice, and yet more by our good examples. You will oblige me to let me hear of her from time to time, and whether she be very fervent and very obedient.

Let us thus think often that our only business in this life is to please God, and that all besides is but folly and vanity. You and I have lived about forty years in religion (i.e., a monastic life). Have we employed them in loving and serving God, who by His mercy has called us to this state, and for that very end? I am filled with shame and confusion when I reflect, on one hand, upon the great favors which God has done, and incessantly continues to do me; and on the other upon the ill use I have made of them, and my small advancement in the way of perfection.

Since by His mercy He gives us still a little time, let us begin in earnest; let us repair the lost time; let us return with a full assurance to that Father of mercies, who is always ready to receive us affectionately. Let us renounce, let us generously re-

nounce, for the love of Him, all that is not Himself;
He deserves infinitely more. Let us think of Him
perpetually. Let us put all our trust in Him. I doubt
not but we shall soon find the effects of it in
receiving the abundance of His grace, with which
we can do all things, and without which we can do
nothing but sin.

We cannot escape the dangers which abound in
life without the actual and *continual* help of God.
Let us, then, pray to Him for it continually. How
can we pray to Him without being with Him? How
can we be with Him but in thinking of Him often?
And how can we often think of Him but by a holy
habit which we should form of it? You will tell me
that I am always saying the same thing. It is true,
for this is the best and easiest method I know; and
as I use no other, I advise all the world to do it.
We must know before we can love. In order to
know God, we must often think of Him; and when
we come to love Him, we shall also think of Him
often, for our heart will be with our treasure. This
is an argument which well deserves your consideration.

> I am,
> Yours . . .

TENTH LETTER

I have had a good deal of difficulty to bring myself to write to Mr.—, and I do it now purely because you and Madam — desire me. Pray write the directions and send it to him. I am very well pleased with the trust which you have in God; I wish that He may increase it in you more and more. We cannot have too much in so good and faithful a Friend, who will never fail us in this world nor in the next.

If Mr.— makes his advantage of the loss he has had, and puts all his confidence in God, He will soon give him another friend, more powerful and more inclined to serve him. He disposes of hearts as He pleases. Perhaps Mr.— was too much attached to him he has lost. We ought to love our friends, but without encroaching upon the love due to God, which must be the principal.

Pray remember what I have recommended to you, which is, to think often on God, by day, by night, in your business, and even in your diversions. He is always near you and with you; leave Him not alone. You would think it rude to leave a friend alone who came to visit you; why, then, must God be neglected? Do not, then, forget Him, but think on Him often, adore Him continually, live and die with Him; this is the glorious employment of a Christian. In a word, this is our profession; if we do not know it, we must learn it. I will endeavor to help you with my prayers, and am, in our Lord,

Yours . . .

ELEVENTH LETTER

I do not pray that you may be delivered from your pains, but I pray God earnestly that He would give you strength and patience to bear them as long as He pleases. Comfort yourself with Him who holds you fastened to the cross. He will loose you when He thinks fit. Happy those who suffer with Him. Accustom yourself to suffer in that manner, and seek from Him the strength to endure as much, and as long, as He shall judge to be necessary for you. The men of the world do not comprehend these truths, nor is it to be wondered at, since they suffer like what they are, and not like Christians. They consider sickness as a pain to nature, and not as a favor from God; and seeing it only in that light, they find nothing in it but grief and distress. But those who consider sickness as coming from the hand of God, as the effect of His mercy, and the means which He employs for their salvation—such commonly find in it great sweetness and sensible consolation.

I wish you could convince yourself that God is often (in some sense) nearer to us, and more effectually present with us, in sickness than in health. Rely upon no other physician; for, according to my apprehension, He reserves your cure to Himself. Put, then, all your trust in Him, and you will soon find the effects of it in your recovery, which we often retard by putting greater confidence in physic than in God.

Whatever remedies you make use of, they will succeed only so far as He permits. When pains come from God, He only can cure them. He often sends diseases of the body to cure those of the soul. Comfort yourself with the sovereign Physician both of the soul and body.

Be satisfied with the condition in which God places you; however happy you may think me, I envy you. Pains and sufferings would be a paradise to me while I should suffer with my God, and the greatest pleasures would be hell to me if I could relish them without Him. All my consolation would be to suffer something for His sake.

I must, in a little time, go to God. What comforts me in this life is that I now see Him by faith; and I see Him in such a manner as might make me say sometimes, *I believe no more, but I see*. I feel what faith teaches us, and in that assurance and that practice of faith I will live and die with Him.

Continue, then, always with God; it is the only support and comfort for your affliction. I shall beseech Him to be with you. I present my service.

I am,

Yours . . .

TWELFTH LETTER

If we were well accustomed to the exercise of the presence of God, all bodily diseases would be much alleviated thereby. God often permits that we should suffer a little to purify our souls and oblige us to continue *with* Him.

Take courage; offer Him your pains incessantly; pray to Him for strength to endure them. Above all, get a habit of entertaining yourself often with God, and forget Him the least you can. Adore Him in your infirmities, offer yourself to Him from time to time, and in the height of your sufferings beseech Him humbly and affectionately (as a child his father) to make you conformable to His holy will. I shall endeavor to assist you with my poor prayers.

God has many ways of drawing us to Himself. He sometimes hides Himself from us; but *faith* alone, which will not fail us in time of need, ought to be our support, and the foundation of our confidence, which must be all in God.

I know not how God will dispose of me. I am always happy. All the world suffer; and I, who deserve the severest discipline, feel joys so continual and so great that I can scarce contain them.

I would willingly ask of God a part of your sufferings, but that I know my weakness, which is so great that if He left me one moment to myself I should be the most wretched man alive. And yet I know not how He can leave me alone, because faith gives me as strong a conviction as sense can do that He never forsakes us until we have first forsaken Him. Let us fear to leave Him. Let us be always with Him. Let us live and die in His presence. Do you pray for me as I for you. I am,

Yours . . .

THIRTEENTH LETTER

(*To the Same*)

I am in pain to see you suffer so long. What gives me some ease and sweetens the feelings I have for your griefs is that they are proofs of God's love toward you. See them in that view and you will bear them more easily. As your case is, it is my opinion that you should leave off human remedies, and resign yourself entirely to the providence of God. Perhaps He stays only for that resignation and a perfect trust in Him to cure you. Since, notwithstanding all your cares, physic has hitherto proved unsuccessful, and your malady still increases, it will not be tempting God to abandon yourself in His hands and expect all from Him.

I told you in my last that He sometimes permits bodily diseases to cure the distempers of the soul. Have courage, then; make a virtue of necessity. Ask of God, not deliverance from your pains, but strength to bear resolutely, for the love of Him, all that He should please, and as long as He shall please.

Such prayers, indeed, are a little hard to nature, but most acceptable to God, and sweet to those that love Him. Love sweetens pains; and when one loves God, one suffers for His sake with joy and courage. Do you so, I beseech you; comfort yourself with Him, who is the only Physician of all our maladies. He is the Father of the afflicted, always ready to help us. He loves us infinitely, more than we imagine. Love Him, then, and seek no consolation elsewhere. I hope you will soon receive it. Adieu. I will help you with my prayers, poor as they are, and shall always be, in our Lord,

Yours . . .

FOURTEENTH LETTER

(To the Same)

I render thanks to our Lord for having relieved you a little, according to your desire. I have been often near expiring, but I never was so much satisfied as then. Accordingly, I did not pray for any relief, but I prayed for strength to suffer with courage, humility and love. Ah, how sweet it is to suffer with God! However great the sufferings may be, receive them with love. It is paradise to suffer and be with Him; so that if in this life we would enjoy the peace of paradise we must accustom ourselves to a familiar, humble, affectionate conversation with Him. We must hinder our spirits' wandering from Him upon any occasion. We must make our heart a spiritual temple, wherein to adore Him incessantly. We must watch continually over ourselves, that we may not do nor say nor think anything that may displease Him. When our minds are thus employed about God, suffering will become full of unction and consolation.

I know that to arrive at this state the beginning is very difficult, for we must act purely in faith. But though it is difficult, we know also that we can do all things with the grace of God, which He never refuses to them who ask it earnestly. Knock, persevere in knocking, and I answer for it that He will open to you in His due time, and grant you all at once what He has deferred during many years. Adieu. Pray to Him for me as I pray to Him for you. I hope to see Him quickly.

I am,

Yours . . .

FIFTEENTH LETTER

(*To the Same*)

God knoweth best what is needful for us, and all that He does is for our good. If we knew how much He loves us, we should always be ready to receive equally and with indifference from His hand the sweet and the bitter. All would please that came from Him. That sorest afflictions never appear intolerable, except when we see them in the wrong light. When we see them as dispensed by the hand of God, when we know that it is our loving Father who abases and distresses us, our sufferings will lose their bitterness and become even matter of consolation.

Let all our employment be to *know* God; the more one knows Him, the more one desires to know Him. And as knowledge is commonly the measure of love, the deeper and more extensive our knowledge shall be, the greater will be our love; and if our love of God were great, we should love Him equally in pains and pleasures.

Let us not content ourselves with loving God for the mere sensible favors, how elevated soever, which He has done or may do us. Such favors, though never so great, cannot bring us so near to Him as faith does in one simple act. Let us seek Him often by faith. He is within us; seek Him not elsewhere. If we do love Him alone, are we not rude, and do we not deserve blame, if we busy ourselves about trifles which do not please and perhaps offend Him? It is to be feared these trifles will one day cost us dear.

Let us begin to be devoted to Him in good earnest. Let us cast everything besides out of our hearts. He would possess them alone. Beg this favor of Him. If we do what we can on our parts, we shall soon see that change wrought in us which we aspire after. I cannot thank Him sufficiently for the relaxation He has vouchsafed you. I hope from His mercy the favor to see Him with a few days.* Let us pray for one another.

> I am, in our Lord,
>
> Yours . . .

---

* He took to his bed two days after, and died within the week.

The

Spiritual

Maxims

of

Brother

Lawrence

INTRODUCTION

Nicholas Herman of Lorraine, a seventeenth-century Carmelite now remembered as Brother Lawrence, is one of those master spirits whose words and influence cannot die. Undoubtedly millions of men and women in the centuries since the Thirty Years' War have found spiritual illumination through the simple but profound insights of Brother Lawrence's famous little book, *The Practice of the Presence of God*.

Now we are indebted to Miss Edith Allais of Hollywood, California, for helping us publish *The Spiritual Maxims of Brother Lawrence*. Miss Allais provided us with a copy of this out-of-print volume and suggested that we republish it. We are happy to be able to do so.

We have no clue to the identity of "H. C." who wrote the original preface, reprinted herewith. Nor do we know to what ancient edition of *The Practice of the Presence of God* the footnotes and page references refer. For the benefit of anyone who may want to check this out, we reproduce it all just as it was previously published.

To all in spiritual quest we commend this book.

THE PUBLISHERS

PREFACE

Brother Lawrence is known to a wide circle of English readers by his "Conversations and Letters," and the numerous editions of that collection are a tribute to the appreciation of the deep spirituality of his teaching. It seems strange therefore that so little attention has been paid to his other writings. The "Spiritual Maxims" appear to have been almost entirely neglected; so far as it can be ascertained no English translation has been published since one at Edinburgh in 1741. It is to atone in some measure for this neglect that the translator offers this new rendering, in full confidence that the many who know Brother Lawrence through the "Conversations" and "Letters" will find here also exemplified the same deep spiritual insight.

The "Spiritual Maxims" were published originally together with the "Letters," the editor of the volume stating in his preface that on running through Brother Lawrence's letters he had found amongst them a manuscript entitled, "Spiritual Maxims, or Means for Attaining to the Presence of God." They deserve attention for two reasons. In a short "Life" of Brother Lawrence, written in 1691, we are told that "he committed his thoughts sometimes to writing, but comparing what he had written with that which he had just experienced in his soul, he deemed it so inferior and so far removed from the inspired thoughts, with which he had been visited, of the greatness and goodness of GOD that often he felt compelled to tear it up at once.'' Apparently the ''Maxims'' and the ''Letters'' are the only writings which have survived. But the ''Maxims'' are important for a further reason. The ''Letters'' were written merely to deal with particular cases and difficulties brought to his notice from time to time, and they were addressed to the individual recipients alone.[1] The ''Maxims,'' however, are in a different category. The careful arrangement adopted suggests matured thought, and the inference is not unreasonable that the intention of Brother Lawrence was to sum up in the ''Maxims'' his teaching, which in the form of letters was inevitably disconnected, in the hope that his message might thereby gain a wider and more general hearing.

The ''Character'' is a sketch of Brother Lawrence as he appeared to those who saw him in the daily round of life. The author is the chronicler of the ''Conversations,'' probably M. Beaufort, grand

[1] ''Letter I.'' p. 27.

N.B.—References in footnotes to the ''Conversations'' and the ''Letters'' of Brother Lawrence relate to the companion edition in this series of *The Practice of the Presence of God*.

vicar to M. de Chalons, Cardinal de Noailles. As far as possible, he allows his subject to speak for himself. "Nobody can paint the Saints so well as they themselves," he writes; "nothing can bring more clearly before you this servant of GOD, than his own words spoken in all the simplicity of his heart."

Under the title of "Gathered Thoughts" the translator has brought together a few scattered sayings of Brother Lawrence which have been collected for the most part from the short "Life" written in 1691. They are only fragments, but well merit being gathered.

Throughout the "Conversations" and the "Letters" there is one great theme which Brother Lawrence develops, the theme which cannot be expressed better than in the words of the Psalmist, "In Thy Presence is fulness of joy." We hear the same melody sounding through this little book—it could not well be otherwise. But is there not another equally insistent on the ear?—"The simplicity that is in Christ."

H. C.

"All things are possible to him who *believes*, they are less difficult to him who *hopes*, they are easier to him who *loves*, and still more easy to him who practices and perseveres in these three virtues."
—BROTHER LAWRENCE

SPIRITUAL MAXIMS

1. We must study ever to regard GOD and His Glory in all that we do, and say, and undertake. This is the *end* that we should set before ourselves, to offer to GOD a sacrifice of perfect worship in this life, as we hope to do through all eternity.[1] We ought firmly to resolve to overcome, with the grace of GOD assisting us, the many difficulties which will meet us in the spiritual life.

2. When we enter upon the spiritual life, we ought to consider thoroughly what we are, probing to the very depth. We shall find that we are altogether deserving of contempt, unworthy of the name of Christ, prone to all manner of maladies and subject to countless infirmities, which distress us and impair the soul's health, rendering us wavering and unstable in our humors and dispositions; in fact, creatures whom it is GOD's will to chasten and make humble by numberless afflictions and adversities, as well within as without.

3. We must believe steadfastly, never once doubting, that such discipline is for our good, that it is GOD's will to visit us with chastening, that it is

[1] "Conversation IV." p. 23.

the course of His Divine Providence to permit our souls to pass through all manner of sore experiences and times of trial, and for the love of God to undergo divers sorrows and afflictions for so long as shall seem needful to Him; since, without this submission of heart and spirit to the will of God, devotion and perfection cannot subsist.

4. A soul is the more dependent on grace, the higher the perfection to which it aspires; and the grace of God is the more needful for each moment, as without it the soul can do nothing. The world, the flesh, and the devil join forces and assault the soul so straitly and so untiringly that, without humble reliance on the ever-present aid of God, they drag the soul down in spite of all resistance. Thus to rely seems hard to nature, but grace makes it become easy, and brings with it joy.

OF NECESSARY PRACTICES FOR ATTAINING TO THE SPIRITUAL LIFE

1. That practice which is alike the most holy, the most general, and the most needful in the spiritual life is *the practice of the Presence of* God. It is *the schooling of the soul to find its joy in His Divine Companionship,* holding with Him at all times and at every moment humble and loving

converse, without set rule or stated method, in all time of our temptation and tribulation, in all time of our dryness of soul and disrelish of God, yes, and even when we fall into unfaithfulness and actual sin.

2. We should apply ourselves unceasingly to this one end, to so rule all our actions that they be little acts of communion with God; but they must not be studied, they must come naturally, from the purity and simplicity of the heart.

3. We must do all things thoughtfully and soberly without impetuosity or precipitancy, which denotes a mind undisciplined. We must go about our labors quietly, calmly, and lovingly, entreating Him to prosper the works of our hands; by thus keeping heart and mind fixed on God, we shall bruise the head of the evil one, and beat down his weapons to the ground.

4. When we are busied, or meditating on spiritual things, even in our time of set devotion, whilst our voice is rising in prayer, we ought to cease for one brief moment, as often as we can, to worship God *in the depth of our being*, to taste Him though it be in passing, to touch Him as it were by stealth. Since you cannot but know that God is with you in all you undertake, that He is at the very depth and centre of your soul, why should you not thus pause an instant from time to time in your outward business, and even in the act of prayer, to worship

Him within your soul, to praise Him, to entreat His aid, to offer Him the service of your heart, and give Him thanks for all His loving-kindnesses and tender-mercies?

What offering is there more acceptable to GOD than thus throughout the day to quit the things of outward sense, and to withdraw to worship Him within the secret places of the soul? Besides by so doing we destroy the love of self, which can subsist only among the things of sense, and of which these times of quiet retirement with GOD rids us well-nigh unconsciously.

In very truth we can render to GOD no greater or more signal proofs of our trust and faithfulness, than by thus turning from things created to find our joy, though for a single moment, in the Creator. Yet, think not that I counsel you to disregard completely and for ever the outward things that are around us. That is impossible. Prudence, the mother of the virtues, must be your guide. Yet, I am confident, it is a common error among religious persons, to neglect this practice of ceasing for a time that, which they are engaged upon, to worship GOD in the depth of their soul, and to enjoy the peace of brief communion with Him. This digression has been long, and yet, it seemed to me, the matter demanded such. Let us return to our subject.

5. These our acts of worship are to be prompted and guided by *faith*. We must unfeignedly believe

that God is in very fact within our souls, and that we must worship Him and love Him and serve Him in spirit and in truth; that He sees all, and that unto Him all hearts are open, our own and those of all His creatures; that He is self-existent, whilst it is in Him that all His creatures live and move and have their being; that His Perfection is Infinite and Sovereign, and demands the full surrender of ourselves, our souls and bodies. In simple justice we owe Him all our thoughts and words and actions. Let us see to it that we pay our debt.

6. Necessity is laid upon us to examine ourselves with diligence to find out what are the virtues, which we chiefly lack, and which are the hardest for us to acquire; we should seek to learn the sins that do most easily beset us, and the times and occasions, when we do most often fall. In the time of struggle we ought to have recourse to God with perfect confidence, abiding steadfast in the Presence of His Divine Majesty; in lowly adoration we should tell out before Him our griefs and our failures, asking Him lovingly for the succor of His grace; and in our weakness we shall find in Him our strength.

OF HOW IT IS REQUIRED OF US TO WORSHIP
GOD IN SPIRIT AND IN TRUTH

There are three points in this question which must be answered:—

1. To worship GOD in spirit and in truth means to offer to Him the worship that we owe. GOD is a Spirit; therefore we must worship Him in spirit and in truth,—that is to say, by presenting to Him a true and humble spiritual worship in the very depth of our being. GOD alone can see this worship, which, offered unceasingly, will in the end become as it were natural, and as if He were one with our soul, and our soul one with Him: practice will make this clear.

2. To worship GOD in truth is to acknowledge Him to be what He is, and ourselves as what in very fact we are. To worship Him in truth is to acknowledge with heart-felt sincerity what GOD in truth is,—that is to say, infinitely perfect, worthy of infinite adoration, infinitely removed from sin, and so of all the Divine attributes. That man is little guided by reason, who does not employ all his powers to render to this great GOD the worship that is His due.

3. Furthermore, to worship GOD in truth is to confess that we live our lives entirely contrary to

His will, and contrary to our knowledge that, were we but willing, He would fain make us conformable to Him. Who will be guilty of such folly as to withhold even for a moment the reverence and the love, the service and the unceasing worship that we owe to Him?

OF UNION OF THE SOUL WITH GOD

There are three degrees of union of the soul with GOD. The first degree is general, the second is virtual union, whilst the third is actual union.

1. That degree of union is the general which one finds, when the soul is united to GOD solely by grace.

2. Virtual union (which is in effect union though not in fact) is our state when, beginning any action by which we are united to GOD, we remain so united to Him by reason of that action for such time as it lasts.

3. Actual union is *the perfect union*. In the other degrees the soul is passive, almost as it were slumbering. In this actual union the soul is intensely active; quicker than fire are its operations, more luminous than the sun, unobscured by any passing cloud. Yet we can be deceived as to this union by our feelings; it is not a mere fleeting emotion, such

as would prompt a passing cry "My God, I love Thee with my heart's full strength"; it is rather a state of soul—if I can but find words—which is deeply spiritual, and yet very simple, which fills us with a joy that is calm indeed, and with a love that is very humble and very reverent, which lifts the soul aloft to heights, where the sense of the love of God constrains it to adore Him, and to embrace Him with a tenderness that cannot be expressed, and which experience alone can teach us to understand.

4. All who aspire to union with the Divine should know that whatever can gladden the will is in fact pleasing to it, or at least so the will reckons it.

There is no one but must avow that God is beyond our understanding. To be united to Him it is needful therefore to deny to the will all tastes and pleasures, bodily and spiritual, that, being thus detached, it can be free to love God above all things. For if the will can in any measure come to know God, it can do so only through *love*.

The difference is great between the tastes and sentiments of the will and its working, since the will's tastes and sentiments are in the soul as in their bounds, whilst its working, which is properly love, finds its sole end in God.

OF THE PRESENCE OF GOD

1. The Presence of GOD is an applying of our spirit to GOD, or a realization of GOD as present, which is borne home to us either by the imagination or by the understanding.

2. I have a friend who these forty years past has been practicing through the understanding a realization of the Presence of GOD. To it he gives many other names; sometimes he calls it a simple *act*, or a clear and distinct *knowledge* of GOD; at other times, a *view* as through a glass, a loving *gaze*, an inward sense of GOD; yet again he terms it a *waiting* on GOD, a silent *converse* with Him, a *repose* in Him, the *life* and *peace* of the soul. Still, my friend tells me that all these ways, in which he has expressed his sense of the Presence of GOD, come to the same thing; and that the Presence fills his soul quite naturally, that it has come so to pass in this way.

3. He says that by unwearying efforts, by constantly recalling his mind to the Presence of GOD, a habit has been formed within him of such a nature that, so soon as he is freed from his ordinary labor, and not seldom even when he is engaged thereon, his soul lifts itself up above all earthly matters, without care or forethought on his part, and dwells as it were firmly stayed on GOD, as in its

centre and place of rest, faith almost always being his companion at such times. Then his soul's joy is full,—it is what he calls the *actual* Presence, and includes all other kinds and greatly more besides. Then it is he feels that only GOD and he are in the world, with Him he holds unbroken converse, asking from Him the supply of all his needs, and finding in His Presence fulness of joy.

4. Let us mark well, however, that this intercourse with GOD he holds *in the depth of his being;* there it is that the soul speaks to GOD, heart to heart, and over the soul thus holding converse there steals a great and profound peace. All that passes without concerns the soul no more than a fire of straw, which the more it flares, the sooner burns itself out; and rarely indeed do the cares of this world ever intrude to trouble the peace that is within.

5. But to come back to our consideration of the Presence of GOD, you must know that the tender and loving light of GOD's countenance kindles insensibly within the soul, which ardently embraces it, so great and so divine a fire of love to GOD, that one is perforce compelled to moderate the outward expression of the feelings.

6. Great would be our surprise, if we but knew what converse the soul holds at these times with GOD, who seems to so delight in this communion, that to the soul, which would fain abide ever with

Him, He bestows favors past numbering; and as if He dreaded lest the soul should turn again to things of earth, He provides for it abundantly, so that the soul finds in faith a nourishment divine, a joy that has no measure, beyond its utmost thought and desire; and this without a single effort on its part but simple consent.

7. The Presence of GOD is thus *the life and nourishment of the soul,* and with the aid of His grace, it can attain thereunto by diligent use of the means which I will now set out.

OF MEANS FOR ATTAINING UNTO THE PRESENCE OF GOD

1. The first is a *great purity of life;* in guarding ourselves with care lest we should do or say or think on anything, which might be displeasing to GOD; and, when any such thing happens, in taking heed to repent thereof, humbly begging His forgiveness.

2. The second is a *great faithfulness in the practice of His Presence,* and in keeping the soul's gaze fixed on GOD in faith, calmly, humbly, lovingly, without allowing an entrance to anxious cares and disquietude.

3. Make it your study, before taking up any task to look to GOD, be it only for a moment, as also

when you are engaged thereon, and lastly when you have performed the same. And forasmuch as without time and great patience this practice cannot be attained, be not disheartened at your many falls; truly this habit can only be formed with difficulty, yet when it is so formed, how great will be your joy therein!

Is it not right that the *heart* which is the first thing in us to have life, and which has dominion over all the body, should be the first and last to love and worship GOD, both when we begin and end our actions, be they spiritual or bodily, and generally in all the affairs of life? It is here therefore, in the heart, that we ought to strive to make a habit of this *gaze* on GOD; but that which is needful to bring the heart to this obedience we must do, as I have already said, quite simply, without strain or study.

4. Those who set out upon this practice let me counsel to offer up in secret a few words, such as "My GOD, I am wholly Thine. O GOD of Love, I love Thee with all my heart. Lord, make my heart even as Thine"; or such other words as love prompts on the instant. But take heed that your mind wanders not back to the world again; keep it fixed on GOD alone, so that, thus subdued by the will, it may be constrained to abide with GOD.

5. This practice of the Presence of GOD is somewhat hard at the outset, yet pursued faithfully,

it works imperceptibly within the soul most marvellous effects; it draws down GOD's grace abundantly, and leads the soul insensibly to the ever-present *vision* of GOD, loving and beloved, which is the most spiritual and most real, the most free and most life-giving manner of prayer.

6. Remember that to attain to this state, we must mortify the senses, inasmuch as no soul, which takes delight in earthly things, can find full joy in the Presence of GOD; to be with Him we must leave behind the creature.

OF THE BENEFITS OF THE PRESENCE OF GOD

1. The first benefit which the soul receives from the Presence of GOD is that *faith grows more alive* and active in all the events of life, particularly when we feel our need, since it obtains for us the succor of His grace when we are tempted, and in every time of trial. Accustomed by this practice to take faith as guide, the soul, by a simple remembrance, sees and feels GOD present, and calls upon Him freely and with assurance of response, receiving the supply of all its needs. By faith, it would seem, the soul draws very near to the state of the Blessed,—the higher it advances, the more living does faith grow, until at last so piercing does the

eye of faith become, that the soul can almost say—*faith* is swallowed up in *sight, I see and I experience*.

2. The practice of the Presence of GOD strengthens us in *hope*. Our hope grows in proportion as our knowledge; and in measure as our faith by this holy practice penetrates into the hidden mysteries of GOD, in like measure it finds in Him a beauty beyond compare, surpassing infinitely that of earth, as also that of the most holy souls and angels. Our hope grows and waxes ever stronger, sustained and enheartened by the fulness of the bliss, which it aspires to and even already tastes in part.

3. Hope breathes into the will a distrust of things seen, and sets it aflame with the consuming fire of Divine love; for GOD's love is in very truth a consuming fire, burning to ashes all that is contrary to His will: the soul thus kindled cannot live save in the Presence of GOD, and this Presence works within the heart a consecrated zeal, a holy ardor, a violent passion to see this GOD known and loved, and served and worshiped by all His creatures.

4. By the practice of the Presence of GOD, by steadfast *gaze* on Him, the soul comes to a knowledge of GOD, full and deep, to *an Unclouded Vision:* all its life is passed in unceasing acts of love and worship, of contrition and of simple trust, of praise and prayer, and service; at times indeed life

seems to be but one long unbroken practice of His Divine Presence.

I know that they are not many who reach this state; it is a grace which GOD bestows only on very few chosen souls, for this Unclouded Vision is a gift from His all-bounteous hand; yet, for the consolation of such as would fain embrace this holy practice, let me say that GOD seldom denies this gift to those who earnestly desire it; and if He do withhold this crowning mercy, be well assured that, by the practice of the Presence of GOD, with the aid of His all-sufficient grace, the soul can attain to a state, which approaches very nearly the Unclouded Vision.

"In these pages you will not find set out a devotion which is merely speculative, or which can only be practiced in a cloister. No, there is an obligation laid on every man to worship GOD and love Him, and we cannot carry out this solemn duty as we ought, unless our heart is knit in love to GOD, and our communion is so close as to constrain us to run to Him at every moment just like little children, who cannot stand upright without their mother's arms of love."
—BEAUFORT

THE CHARACTER OF
BROTHER LAWRENCE

BEING THE TEACHING OF HIS LIFE

I am writing down what I have heard and seen myself of the ''Character'' of Brother Lawrence, who died about two years ago in the Carmelite Monastery at Paris, and whose memory is a sweet savor.

One, who has chosen to be a doorkeeper in the house of GOD rather than hold a high rank among sinners, who has taken upon him the yoke of JESUS CHRIST, and preferred it to the empty pomp and pleasures of the world, has asked me to write down for those souls, who have been freed from the chain of things seen, what he knew I had collected of the thoughts and precepts of Brother Lawrence. Willingly I obey, and although a sketch of the ''Life'' and a collection of the ''Letters'' of this good Brother have been already published, it seems to me that we cannot make known too widely what we have preserved of this holy man. It is my firm belief that I can do no greater service than by holding up this man as a pattern of solid piety in an age, when almost every one puts virtue where it is not, and takes false ways to arrive at it.

It will be Brother Lawrence himself who will speak in these pages. In the "Conversations," which I had with him, I will give you his own words, just as I wrote them down straightway on leaving him. Nobody can paint the Saints so well as they themselves. The "Confessions and Letters of St. Augustine" give us a far more living portrait than anything that man could have added. So nothing can bring more clearly before you this servant of GOD than his own words spoken in all the simplicity of his heart.

With all his virtue Brother Lawrence was intensely human; he had a frank open manner, which, when you met him, won your confidence at once, and made you feel that you had found a friend, to whom you could unbosom yourself wholly.

On his part, directly he knew with whom he was dealing, he spoke quite freely and gave immediate proof of his great goodness of heart. What he said was very simple, but to the point, and full of sense. Behind a rather rough exterior, one found a singular sagacity, a spaciousness of mind quite beyond the range of the ordinary poor lay brother, a penetration that surpassed all expectation. As a man of affairs he was capable of carrying through the greatest matters, and of giving wise and safe counsel. Such were the characteristics that struck the ordinary observer.

The disposition of his heart, and the inner life of his soul, he has himself depicted in the "Conversations'' which I am going to give you. His conversion sprung from a high notion, which he conceived of the power and wisdom of God, Whom ever afterwards he sought diligently and with great faithfulness, driving away all other thoughts.

As this first realization of God was the beginning of the perfection of Brother Lawrence, for so it has proved to be, it is important that we should stop here for a little, to consider his conduct at this time. *Faith* was the one light he took for his path; not only did it afford him his first glimpse of God, but he never desired any other lamp to give him light in all the many ways of God. Often he has told me that ''all that he had heard others say, all that he had found in books, all that he had himself written, seemed savorless, dull and heavy, when compared with what faith had unfolded to him of the unspeakable riches of God and of Jesus Christ. He alone,'' he continued, ''can reveal Himself to us; we toil and exercise our mind in reason and in science, forgetting that therein we can see only a copy, whilst we neglect to gaze on the Incomparable Original. In the depths of our soul, God reveals Himself, could we but realize it, yet we will not look there for Him. We leave Him to spend our time in fooleries, and affect disdain at commune with Him, Who is ever-present, Who is our King.

''It is not enough to know God as a *theory*, from

what we read in books, or feel some fleeting motions of affection for Him, brief as the wave of feeling, or glimpse of the Divine, which prompts them; our faith must be alive, and we must make it so, and by its means lift ourselves beyond all these passing emotions to worship the FATHER and JESUS CHRIST in all their Divine Perfection. This path of faith is the spirit of the Church, and will lead to a great perfection."

Not only did Brother Lawrence perceive GOD as present in his soul by faith, but in all the events of life, whensoever they befell, instantly he would arise and seek the Presence of GOD.

A leafless tree he saw in winter first flashed in upon his soul the *fact* of GOD; so great and so sublime was the vision that after forty years it was as clear and vivid as when he first received it. Such was his practice, throughout life, using things seen to lead him up to the Unseen Eternal.

In his reading, Brother Lawrence far preferred above all other books the Holy Gospel, inasmuch as he found that he could nourish his faith more simply and more purely in the very words of JESUS CHRIST.

Thus it was that Brother Lawrence set out upon the spiritual life, with firm resolve, faithfully pursued, to foster in his heart this sublime sense of the Presence of GOD, as seen through faith. Therein he continued steadfastly, glorifying GOD, and showing his love to Him in ways past number. In all he undertook, he entreated the aid of Our Lord, giving thanks after he had performed the same; and, having confessed his negligences, he asked pardon therefor trustfully, without, as he termed it, pleading with God. And forasmuch as this communion with God was interwoven with his daily labor, and furnished him with matter for it, he did his work with the greater ease, and very far from distracting him, it aided him therein.

Yet he confessed that it was hard at first, that many a time he had been unmindful of this practice, but that, after humble confession of his failure, he had betaken himself to it again without trouble.

At times a crowd of wandering wild fancies would invade his mind and take violent possession of the place of God; when such happened, he told me, he kept quite calm, and proceeded straightway to expel them; this done, he returned to his commune with God.

At last his faithfulness and patience won its reward, in the possession of his soul by a sense, unbroken and undisturbed, of the Presence of God. All his acts, in kind so varying and so multiplied in number, were changed into an unclouded vision, an illumined love, a joy uninterrupted.

This is what he once told me: "For me the time of action does not differ from the time of prayer, and in the noise and clatter of my kitchen, while several persons are together calling for as many different things, I possess GOD in as great tranquillity as when upon my knees as the Blessed Sacrament. Sometimes, indeed, my faith becomes so clear that I almost fancy that I have lost it,—the shadows which veil our vision usually seem to be fleeing away, and there begins to dawn that day which is to be without cloud and without end, the glorious day of the life to come.''

To such heights as these faithfulness led our good Brother, that faithfulness which bade him cast behind all other thoughts to leave his soul free for unbroken communion with GOD. And in the end, so much did habit become second nature, that, as he told me, it was in a manner impossible for him to turn away from GOD, and busy himself with other matters.

In the ''Conversations''[1] he makes an observation on this point which is important; I mean, when he says, that the Presence of GOD can be reached rather by the heart and by love than by the understanding,—these are his words: ''In the way of GOD *thoughts* count for little, *love* is everything.

''Nor is it needful,'' he goes on to say, ''that we should have great things to do.'' I am giving you a picture of a lay brother serving in a kitchen; let me then use his own words: ''We can do *little* things for GOD; I turn the cake that is frying on the pan for the

[1] ''Conversation II.'' p. 16.

love of Him, and that done, if there is nothing else to call me, I prostrate myself in worship before Him, Who has given me grace to work; afterwards I rise happier than a king. It is enough for me to pick up but a straw from the ground for the love of GOD.

"We search for stated ways and methods of learning how to love GOD, and to come at that love we disquiet our minds by I know not how many devices; we give ourselves a world of trouble and pursue a multitude of practices to attain to a sense of the Presence of GOD. And yet it is so simple. How very much shorter it is and easier to do our *common business* purely *for the love of* GOD, to set His consecrating mark on all we lay hands to, and thereby to foster the sense of His abiding Presence by communion of our *heart* with His! There is no need either of art or science; just as we are, we can go to Him, simply and with single heart." I preserve His words religiously.

We must not, however, fancy that to learn to love GOD it suffices to offer Him our acts and entreat His aid and show forth works of love. Brother Lawrence only attained to the perfection of his love, because from the very outset he had laid stern discipline upon himself to do nothing which might be displeasing to GOD, and because forgetting self, he had renounced all for His sake. Here are his very words: "Since entering upon the religious life, I no longer perplex myself with thoughts of virtue, or of my salvation.

But having given myself wholly to GOD, to make what satisfaction I could for my sins, and for love of Him having renounced all that is not His, I have come to see that my only business is to live as though there were none but He and I in the world.''

Thus Brother Lawrence began by what was most perfect, forsaking all for GOD, and doing everything for His love. He entirely forgot self: he never any longer thought on heaven or hell or on his past sins, nor on those he daily committed, after he had asked GOD's forgiveness of them. Having confessed them, he no more suffered his mind to go back thereon, but, with the confession, entered upon a perfect peace; after which he commended himself to GOD, as he used to say, for life and for death, for time and for eternity.

We are *made for* GOD, and for Him, alone; He cannot therefore take it ill that we forsake all, even ourselves, to find our *all in Him*. In GOD we shall see more clearly what we lack than we could in ourselves by all our introspection; which in reality is but the remnant, unexpelled, of self-love, which, under the guise of zeal for our own perfection, keeps our gaze down on self instead of raised to GOD.

Brother Lawrence often said that during these four years of his life,[1] those years of trial, when no

---

[1] ''Conversation II.'' p. 12.

one could lift from his soul the burdening sense that
he was lost, he had never wavered in his first
determination; that instead of vainly attempting to
pierce the future, and as vainly dwelling upon the
present anguish of his mind, as do most troubled
souls, he used to console himself with some such
thought as this—"Let what may come of it, however many be the days remaining to me, I will do all
things for the love of GOD"; that thus in *forgetting
self* he had in truth *found God*.

He told me that in his soul he had found that love
for the will of GOD had taken the place of that which
a man ordinarily has for his own; in all the events of
life he saw plainly the workings of the Divine Will,
and this kept him in perfect peace, because his mind
was stayed on GOD. When he was told of any great
wickedness, he was not a whit surprised; rather, he
would say, he marvelled not to hear of more, when
he considered the baseness into which sin leads a
man; that for his part he rose straightway to the
throne of GOD, and forasmuch as He could remedy
such, yet permitted evil for reasons very true and
useful in the order of His Providence, he prayed and
interceded for the sinner, and, having done so,
continued in His peace.

One day I remember telling him without any
forewarning that a matter of great consequence to
him, and one, on which he had set his heart and
long labored for, could not be carried out, as the

superiors had just made up their minds against it. Quite simply he replied, "We must believe they have good reasons for their decision, and our duty now is to obey, and say no more about it." He did so indeed himself, and though he had many occasions to speak of it afterwards, he not so much as opened his mouth thereon.

Once when Brother Lawrence was very ill, a man of great sanctity of life[1] came to visit him, and asked him which he would choose, if GOD permitted him, whether to live a little longer to grow in holiness, or to receive him at once into heaven. The good Brother never hesitated; he replied that he would leave the choice to GOD; that as for himself he had nothing else to do but to wait in peace, till GOD should show him what was His will.

This disposition brought him to so great an indifference about everything, and to such perfect freedom, that it was very like the freedom of the Blessed. He had no bias; not a trace of self could one discover in his character, nor of any prejudice arising from those natural attachments which men commonly possess. He was beloved equally of those of the most contrary temperaments. He wished well to all, without respect of persons. Citizen of Heaven, nothing could hold him chained to earth; his vision was not bordered by time; from

[1] Fénélon, Archbishop of Cambrai.

long contemplation of Him, Who is Eternal, he had become himself like Him.

Everything came alike to him, every station, every duty. The good Brother found GOD everywhere, as near when he was at the humblest task as when praying with the Community. He found no urgency for retreats, inasmuch as in the common task he met the same GOD to love and worship, as in the stillness of the desert.

His one method of going to GOD and abiding in His Presence was *to do all for the love of Him*. It was a matter of no consequence to him, whether he was employed on one thing or the other, provided that therein he sought GOD's glory. It was to Him he looked, and not to the work in hand. He knew that the more opposed the task was to his inclination, the greater and more blessed was the love which made him sacrifice his will to GOD; that the *littleness* of the work lessened not one whit the value of the offering, for GOD *regards not the greatness of the work, but the love which prompts it*.

Another quality one marked in Brother Lawrence was his singular firmness of mind, such as in another walk of life one would have called dauntlessness, which gave proof of a noble soul raised far beyond the fear and hope of all that was not GOD. He marvelled at nothing, nothing astonished him or gave him cause for fear. This stability of soul sprung from the same source as did all his other virtues. The high notion which he had of GOD revealed in his heart a perfect picture of his Creator in all His Sovereign Justice and Infinite Mercy. Resting on this he was assured that GOD would never deceive him, and would send such things only as were good for him, forasmuch as on his part he was resolved never to grieve Him, but to do and suffer all for love of Him.

One day I asked him who was his "director." He answered, he had none, and that he believed he needed none; for the rule and office of his state marked out for him his path in outward matters, as the Gospel did the obligation of the inner life of loving GOD with all his heart; that knowing this a "director" did not seem needful, but he had great want of a "confessor."

Those who take no other guidance in the spiritual life but their *particular dispositions and feelings,* who fancy that they have nothing more important to do than to examine themselves as to whether they *feel* devout or not, such can have no stability nor any certain rule; because our dispositions change continually, sometimes owing to our own sloth, sometimes by the ordinance of GOD, Who varies His gifts towards us according to our needs.

Our good Brother, on the other hand, kept steadfastly in the *Way of Faith,* which never changes; he was ever constant, for the reason that his one study was to carry out the duties of the station wherein GOD had placed him, counting nothing commendable but the virtues of that station. Instead of watching his dispositions or stopping to test the way in which he walked, he fixed his gaze on GOD alone, the Goal of his race, and *sped* along towards Him by daily acts of meekness and righteousness and love. He set himself to do, rather than to reflect on what to do.

The devotion of Brother Lawrence, resting on this solid base, was not given to fantasies. He was convinced that such as are genuine are most often signs of feebleness in a soul, which is content rather with GOD's gifts than with Himself. From the time of his novitiate, there was nothing of this in his conduct, at least nothing was heard or seen of it by those who had his confidence, and to whom he commonly unbosomed himself.

All his days he followed in the footprints of the Saints, along the sure and certain path of faith. He strayed not from the beaten track, which leads to salvation by the practice of those virtues, which the Church has declared from the beginning; at all else he looked askance. His great common-sense and the light afforded by his simple faith warned him of those sunken rocks, which one finds in the spiritual life, and on which so many souls make shipwreck, letting themselves drift along the current of curiosity and imagination, of love of novelty and human guidance. Yet nothing is easier than to avoid these perils when we seek GOD alone. In the matter of religion, what is new needs careful examination, inasmuch as virtue is not of the number of things, which grow slowly to perfection, but, on the contrary, is perfect from the very first.

Prepared by such a life, Brother Lawrence saw death draw near without perturbation. His patience had been great indeed through all his life, but it waxed stronger ever as he approached the end. He was never in the least fretful, when he was most wracked with pain; joy was manifest not only on his countenance, but still more in his speech, so much so in fact that those who visited him were constrained to ask whether he was not suffering. "Forgive me," he replied. "Yes, I do suffer, the pains in my side sore trouble me, but my spirit is happy and well content." They added, "Suppose GOD will that you suffer for ten years, what then?" "I would suffer," he answered, "not for ten years only, but till the Day of Judgment, if it be GOD's will; and I would hope that He would continue to aid me with His grace to bear it joyfully."

His one desire was that he might suffer something for the love of GOD, for all his sins, and finding in his last illness a favorable occasion for suffering in this life, he embraced it heartily. Purposely he bade the brethren to turn him on to his right side; he knew that this position gave great pain, and therefore wished to remain therein to satisfy his burning desire to suffer. A brother, who was watching at his bed, wished to relieve him in some measure; but twice he answered, "I thank you, my dear brother, but I beg of you to let me bear just a little for the love of GOD." Often in the hour of pain he would cry out with fervor, "My GOD I worship Thee in my infirmities. Now, now, I shall have something to bear for Thee,—good, be it so, may I suffer and die with Thee." Then he would repeat those verses of the fifty-first Psalm, *"Create in me a clean heart, O GOD. Cast me not away from Thy Presence. Restore unto me the joy of Thy salvation."* [1]

As the hour when he was to leave this life drew near, he exclaimed frequently, *"Oh, faith, faith"*; this was indeed more expressive of his life than any longer utterance could be. His worship of GOD never ceased: he told a brother of the Community that he hardly needed *faith* any longer to realize GOD present in his soul, for already faith was well-nigh swallowed up in *sight*.

So amazing was his boldness in that dark valley, from which so many shrink, that he told one, who had asked him, that he feared neither death nor hell, neither the judgment of GOD nor the attacks of the evil one.

His words were so full of comfort and of grace

[1] This paragraph is taken from the short "Life" of Brother Lawrence.

that many of the brethren questioned him. One of them asked him, if he knew how terrible a thing it was to fall into the hands of the living GOD, inasmuch as no man, whoever he be, knows for certain whether he deserves GOD's love or not. "I agree," said Brother Lawrence, "but I should not wish to know it, for fear of vanity; we can do nothing better than abandon ourselves to GOD."

After he had received the last Sacraments, a brother asked him if he were easy and what his mind was busied with. This was the reply: "I am doing what I shall do, through all eternity—blessing GOD, praising GOD, adoring GOD, giving Him the love of my whole heart. It is our *one business*, my brethren, *to worship Him and love Him*, without thought of anything else."

One of the Community having commended himself to Brother Lawrence's prayers, and having begged him to entreat of GOD for him the true spirit of prayer, he replied that there was need of labor on his part also to make himself worthy of such a gift.

These were his last words. On the morrow, which was Monday, the 12th of February 1691, at nine o'clock in the morning, without any pain or struggle, without losing in the slightest the use of any of his faculties, Brother Lawrence passed away in the embrace of his LORD, and rendered his soul to GOD in the peace and calm of one who had fallen on sleep.

Nothing can give a clearer picture of a true Christian philosophy *in practice* than the life and death of this good Brother,—yet another of that band, who from times of old have forsaken the world to dedicate with single heart their powers to cultivate the life of the spirit, and to come to a knowledge of GOD and of His SON JESUS CHRIST,—devoted souls, who have taken the Gospel as their only rule, and have faithfully professed the holy Philosophy of the Cross.

It is thus that *S. Clement of Alexandria* describes them in the Seventh Book of the "Stromata." It would seem that he had in view a man just like Brother Lawrence, when he said that the great business of a philosopher, that is, a wise Christian, is *prayer*. Such an one prays in every place, at every time, not indeed using many words, or thinking to be heard for his much speaking, but in secret in the depths of his soul, while walking or conversing with his fellow-men, or reading, at the table, when at work. His praises rise to GOD unceasingly; not only in the morning, and at noon, but in all his actions he glorifies GOD as do the Seraphim. Continual contemplation through prayer on spiritual things makes him meek, gentle, patient, whilst strong as iron to battle with temptation, giving no hold upon himself, either to pleasure or to sorrow.

The joy of contemplation on which he feeds unceasingly, without being satiated, renders him insensible to all empty pleasures. He dwells by *love* with GOD, and having seen through *faith* a vision of the *Light of Lights*, he has no taste for what the world can offer. Through love he has attained already what he lacks, and he longs for nought, because, so far as in this life he can, he has the *Object* of his heart's desire.

He has no ground for fear, inasmuch as nothing in this life can hurt him, nor turn his heart from the love of GOD. He has no need to school his spirit into calmness, seeing that his mind is at rest, persuaded that all things work together for good. Nothing perturbs him, and anger he knows not, because of the love he has to GOD. Jealousy can gain no entrance, inasmuch as he lacks nothing. He loves his fellowmen with no mere human fondness, but as the objects of the love of a loved and loving Father. His spirit is steadfast and unchangeable, for he has committed all his ways unto GOD and rests on Him alone.

I should like to add to this portrait a finishing touch from the hand of a great master, one who was more illumined by the light of that *faith* which he had in common with Brother Lawrence than by all the science and philosophy of Greece. Will anyone find fault with me for ranking together the great Masters and Doctors with an obscure lay brother, when one finds in his simple words and life the same full purity and perfection of Christian precept and practice, which the greatest lights of the Church have handed down to us, and which all alike have drawn from JESUS CHRIST, Who hides Himself from those who in their own imaginations are wise and prudent, revealing Himself to the humble and lowly of heart?

No one can be more brave or dauntless, says *S. Gregory of Nazianzus* ("Orat. 28"), than the true Christian philosopher. Everything gives way to his largeness of heart; if one denies him all that earth can give, he has wings wherewith to fly, and find his refuge in GOD. He knows no limits; he lives on earth as a man wholly in heaven, unmoved amid the storm of passions. He yields in everything, save in the greatness of his courage, and by yielding he surpasses those who fancy to eclipse him.

He uses the supports of life ("Orat. 29") no further than necessity obliges him. His only intercourse is with GOD. Raised above all things of outward sense, his soul is a stainless, spotless mirror, reflecting the Divine without any intermingling of what is gross and earthly. Daily he adds new lights of virtue to those he has already, until at length he comes unto Him, Who is the *Fountain of Light*, in Whose Light he shall indeed see light, when the Glory of Truth shall have scattered the darkness of all enigmas in the day of perfect Bliss. In this one recognizes our lay brother, and all of like mind and heart.

Though it was in a very lowly corner that Brother Lawrence lived his days, yet there is no person, of whatsoever station or condition he be, who may not draw great profit from his life.

Those who are filled with the cares of this world he will teach to draw near to God, to ask from Him the grace to do their duty faithfully, never forgetting that they can approach God, when they are most busied, in the market, and where men do congregate, or in the hour of leisure. By the example of our good Brother, they will be moved to render thanks to God for all His mercies, and for the good that He inspires them to do, humbling themselves before Him for their many failures.

In these pages they will not find set out a devotion which is merely speculative, or which can only be practiced in a cloister. No, there is an obligation laid on every man to worship God and love Him, and we cannot carry out this solemn duty as we ought, unless our heart is knit in love to God, and our communion is so close as to constrain us to run to Him at every moment, just like little children, who cannot stand upright without their mother's arms of love.

Far from this communion with our Father being difficult, it is very easy, and very necessary for every one; it is to this that *S. Paul* says that all Christians are constrained. Whoever does not practice it, whoever does not feel his great necessity, whoever does not grasp his total inability alone to do aright, is ignorant of his own self, ignorant of

GOD his Father, utterly ignorant of his *continual need* of JESUS CHRIST.

No affairs or cares of the world can serve as an excuse for neglecting this our duty. GOD is everywhere, in all places, and there is no spot where we cannot draw near to Him, and hear Him speaking in our heart; with a little *love*, just a very little, we shall not find it hard.

Such as are withdrawn from the embarrassments and perplexities of life have still greater opportunities of following in the steps of Brother Lawrence. Freed for the most part from the ambitions and conventions of the world, which give to those struggling in its throng most of their cares and troubles, there is nothing to hinder them from taking the example of our good Brother, and renouncing all desire other than that of living every moment of their life, and doing every action for the love of GOD, giving to Him—in Brother Lawrence's own words[1]—the *all* for the *all*.

The example of his complete detachment from the world, of his entire forgetfulness of self, which led him to think no longer even of his salvation to keep his mind free for GOD to fill, of his indifference to what life might bring, and of his freedom in the spiritual life, cannot fail to be fraught with blessing beyond measure.

[1] "Letter I." p. 28.

"Believe me, count as lost each day you have not used in loving GOD."—BROTHER LAWRENCE

GATHERED THOUGHTS

It matters not to me what I do, or what I suffer, so long as I abide lovingly united to GOD's will,—that is my whole *business*.

I am in the hands of GOD, and He has His own good purposes regarding me; therefore I trouble not myself for aught that man can do to me. If I cannot serve GOD here, elsewhere I shall find a place wherein to serve Him.

The practice of the Presence of GOD is the shortest and easiest *Way* to attain *to Christian perfection:* it is *the Form and Life of Virtue*, it is the great *Preservative from Sin*. The practice will become easy, if we have but courage and a good will.

The whole world seems to me to be no longer real; all that my outward eyes behold pass like fantasies and dreams. That which I see with the eyes of the soul is what alone I long for, and to be not yet in the possession of my heart's desire brings to me sorrow and drooping of spirit. On the one hand dazzled by the brightness of the Sun of Righteousness, the Scatterer of the shades of night, and, on the other, with eyes dimmed by my own sin, I feel at times as if I were beside myself. And yet, I make it my ordinary business to abide in the

Presence of God with the humility of a useless, though a faithful servant.

Since I first entered on the religious life, I have looked on God as the *Goal* and *End* of all the thoughts and affections of the soul. As a novice, during the hours appointed for prayer I labored to arrive at a conviction of the truth of the Divine Being, rather by the light of faith than by the deductions of the intellect, and by this short and certain method I grew in the knowledge of this *Object* of Love, in Whose Presence I resolved evermore to abide. Possessed thus entirely with the greatness and the majesty of this Infinite Being, I went straightway to the place which duty had marked out for me—the kitchen. There, when I had carried out all that called for me, I gave to prayer whatever time remained, as well before my work as after. Before beginning any task I would say to God, with childlike trust: "O God, since Thou art with me, and it is Thy will that I must now apply myself to these outward duties, I beseech Thee, assist me with Thy grace that I may continue in Thy Presence; and to this end, O Lord, be with me in this my work, accept the labor of my hands, and dwell within my heart with all Thy Fulness." Moreover, as I wrought, I would continue to hold familiar converse, offering to Him my little acts of service, entreating the unfailing succor of His grace. When I had finished, I would examine how I had performed my duty: if I found well, I gave Him thanks; if ill, I besought His pardon, and without losing heart I set my spirit right, and returned anew unto His Presence, as though I had never wandered from Him. Thus, by rising after every fall, and by doing all in faith and love, without wearying, I have come to a state in which it would be as little possible for me not to think of GOD, as it was hard to discipline myself thereto at the beginning.

O LORD, O GOD of gods, how wonderful Thou art in all Thy thoughts, beyond our understanding, how profound in all Thy purposes, Almighty in the works of Thy Hands!

All that I have heard men tell concerning GOD, that I have read myself, or perceived of Him in my mind, cannot content me. Infinite in His Perfection, how can He be portrayed, or how can man find words to picture Him? Faith alone can reveal Him or teach me what He is; by faith I learn more of GOD, and in a very little time, than I could do in the schools after many a long year. Oh! Faith, faith; oh! marvellous virtue, which illumines the spirit of man, and leads him on to the knowledge of his Creator. Oh! virtue altogether lovely, so little known, and still less practiced, yet which, once known, is so glorious, so full of unspeakable Blessing.

The greatest glory we can give to GOD is to

distrust our own strength utterly, and to commit ourselves wholly to His safe-keeping.

O LORD, the sense of Thy love well-nigh over-whelms me. If it be Thy will, bestow these many tokens of Thy loving-kindness on those who know Thee not, to draw them to Thy service; for me it is enough to have the riches that faith brings in the knowledge of Thee. Yet forasmuch as I must not reject the favors of Thy bounteous Hand, accept my praises, LORD. And, I entreat, receive again these gifts, which Thou hast granted; for, LORD, Thou knowest that it is not Thy gifts I seek, but Thee Thyself, and my heart will know no rest, till it has found Thee.

O LORD, enlarge the chambers of my heart that I may find room for Thy love. Sustain me by Thy power, lest the fire of Thy love consume me.

The practice of the Presence of GOD is of very great service in helping us to pray in truth; it restrains the mind from wandering throughout the day and holds it fixed steadfastly on GOD; thus it will more easily remain tranquil in the hour of prayer.

Life is full of perils and of hidden reefs, on which we shall make shipwreck without the continual succor of the grace of GOD. Yet how can we ask for it, unless we are with Him? How can we be with Him, unless our thoughts are ever of Him? How can He be in our thoughts, unless we form a holy habit of abiding in His Presence, there asking for the grace we need each moment of our life?

If you would go forward in the spiritual life, you must avoid relying on the subtle conclusions and fine reasonings of the unaided intellect. Unhappy they who seek to satisfy their desire therein! The Creator is the great teacher of Truth. We can reason laboriously for many years, but fuller far and deeper is the knowledge of the hidden things of faith and of Himself, which He flashes as light into the *heart* of the *humble*.

Nothing can give us so great relief in the trials and sorrows of life, as a loving intercourse with GOD; when such is faithfully practiced, the evils that assail the body will prove light to us. GOD often ordains that we should suffer in the body to purify the soul, and to constrain us to abide with Him. How can anyone whose life is hid with GOD, and whose only desire is GOD, be capable of feeling pain? Let us then worship Him in our infirmities, offering to Him our sorrows, just when they press upon us, asking Him lovingly, as a child his dear father, to give us strength, and mold our will to His. Brief prayers as these are very proper for all sick persons, and prove a wonderful charm against sorrow.

Ah, did I know that my heart loved not GOD, this very instant I would pluck it out.

O Loving-Kindness so old and still so new, I

have been too late of loving Thee. You are young, my brethren; profit therefore I beseech you from my confession, that I cared too little to employ my early years for GOD. Consecrate all yours to His Love. If I had only known Him sooner, if I had only had some one to tell me then what I am telling you, I should not have so long delayed in loving Him. Believe me, count as lost each day you have not used in loving GOD.